FIGHTING FOR THE CIVIL RIGHTS ACT OF 1964

A HISTORY SEEKING ADVENTURE

by Elliott Smith

CAPSTONE PRESS
a capstone imprint

Published by You Choose, an imprint of Capstone
1710 Roe Crest Drive, North Mankato, Minnesota 56003
capstonepub.com

Library of Congress Cataloging-in-Publication Data is available on the Library of
Congress website.

ISBN: 9781669058281 (hardcover)
ISBN: 9781669058250 (paperback)
ISBN: 9781669058267 (ebook PDF)

Summary: YOU are fighting for equity and equal rights during the turbulent
1960s. How will you take part in this historic battle? Will you join the Freedom
Riders to fight segregation on buses? Will you sit in at segregated lunch counters
or join the March on Washington for Jobs and Freedom? Step back in time to take
part in this historic fight for equality.

Editorial Credits
Editor: Mandy Robbins; Designer: Heidi Thompson; Media Researcher: Jo Miller;
Production Specialist: Tori Abraham

Image Credits
Alamy: Everett Collection Historical, 95; Associated Press, 23, Henry Burroughs,
51; Getty Images: Afro Newspaper/Gado, 43, Bettmann, 4, 11, Central Press, 17,
48, Don Uhrbrock, 33, Hulton Archive, 39, 99, Michael Ochs Archives, 73, 75, 91,
MPI, 63, 85, Pictorial Parade, 68; Library of Congress, 55; Shutterstock: Michael
Gordon, 81; Wikimedia: LBJ Presidential Library, 105, NARA, Cover

All internet sites appearing in back matter were available and accurate when this
book was sent to press.

TABLE OF CONTENTS

ABOUT YOUR ADVENTURE

YOU are living during the 1960s. Slavery ended nearly 100 years earlier, but for many Black people like you, life isn't much better. Minorities across the country, especially in the South, struggle with inequality and poor treatment. Jim Crow laws have turned many Black people into second-class citizens.

You want to change this, so you join the Civil Rights Movement. People in this movement want to end segregation. You want equal rights to jobs, housing, and voting for all people. What part will you play in the fight for civil rights?

Explore several key campaigns in the battle for equality. Some choices mean the difference between life and death. The events you experience happened to real people, both famous and forgotten.

Chapter One introduces the story. Then YOU CHOOSE which path to read. Follow the directions at the bottom of each page. The choices you make will change your outcome. After you finish one path, go back and read the others for new perspectives and more adventures.

Turn the page to begin your adventure.

CHAPTER 1

THE QUEST FOR EQUALITY

As a Black person living in the United States in the 1960s, equality seems like a dream. Racism is part of your everyday life. In the North, restrictive housing laws limit the places where minorities can live.

Jim Crow laws are common throughout the South. These rules restrict Black life in a variety of ways. "Separate but equal" is the norm. From train stations to lunch counters, Black and white people are kept away from each other. But the facilities used by Black people are always worse.

Turn the page.

Voting rights are another major concern. Poll taxes, literacy tests, and voter intimidation have all but stripped Black people of their voting rights, especially in the South. Political leaders don't want Black voters to register.

You're hopeful that things will change. A new wave of leaders is working hard to ensure civil rights for all. You've read in the newspaper about Dr. Martin Luther King Jr., a young minister from Atlanta. You've seen young people, both Black and white, on TV, marching and protesting. It's inspiring. But it's also a little scary. People are getting hurt. Others are getting arrested. You think it's a risk worth taking. You're ready to join the fight for civil rights.

- To join the Freedom Riders fighting segregation on buses, turn to page 13.

- To join the Birmingham Campaign in America's most segregated city, turn to page 53.

- To participate in the March on Washington for Jobs and Freedom, turn to page 83.

Reverend Dr. Martin Luther King Jr. and Reverend Ralph Abernathy in jail

CHAPTER 2

THE ROAD TO FREEDOM

It is 1961, and you're a Black college student in Atlanta. You've tried to focus on your studies, but it's hard to ignore the movement building in the city around equality and civil rights. Graduation is only a few months away, but you're starting to feel the pull of the cause.

You deal with racism daily. You can't sit at the local lunch counter. You have to sit in the balcony at the movie theater. People are frustrated and angry at the inequality. But now, you have real hope that change is in the air.

Turn the page.

Groups such as the Congress of Racial Equality (CORE) and the Student Nonviolent Coordinating Committee (SNCC) have started making plans. They want to disrupt local Jim Crow laws.

Your friends have started talking about fighting segregation on public transportation. The Supreme Court has handed down two rulings stating that segregated buses and bus stations were unconstitutional. Yet, it's still understood that Black riders must head for the back of the bus. Your friends plan to challenge this unwritten rule. They're calling themselves Freedom Riders. It's sure to upset some people, and it could be dangerous.

"Come on, let's sign on for the rides," your friend Mary says. "They're going to be stopping in Atlanta soon. It's a chance for us to make a real difference in the community."

One part of you is eager to jump in and help. Another part of you hesitates. Your parents are worried about this movement. They have warned you to be careful. Perhaps you should see if anything dangerous happens before you join up.

• To join the Freedom Riders now, turn to page 16.

• To wait and join up later in the campaign, turn to page 34.

When you arrive to the meetup at a local church, you are surprised to see a diverse group of people. Black and white people are talking and laughing with each other. Mary nudges you and says, "Let's get a seat up front."

After a few minutes, a couple of well-dressed men stand in front of the seats. The first one steps forward.

"For those of you who don't know me, my name is Charles Person," he says. "I am one of the riders. I have worked with John Lewis and James Farmer with SNCC and CORE. We've stopped here on our bus ride to New Orleans."

You look around and see confident nods from the people who have already taken rides. The newcomers look a little nervous.

"Let's break into smaller groups," Charles says. "Newcomers over here."

CORE demonstrators at the 1964 World's Fair

You go with several other people. It's a mix of old and young, Black and white. Charles strides over to the group.

Turn the page.

"Let me tell you a little about our plan," he says. "We have one Black person and one white person per seat. Our policy is nonviolent protest. That means, even if we're attacked, we don't fight back. If violence erupts, we're likely to get arrested for breach of peace, but that's okay. We want the public to see the jails filled with people who haven't broken any laws. Eventually, the federal government will have to step in. They'll have to force these states to accept that segregation is illegal."

You swallow as Charles details some of the encounters the riders have experienced and what lies ahead on the journey. He says that the riders shouldn't expect any help from the police. They may even encounter the Ku Klux Klan. This violent group of white men in robes and hoods is responsible for many attacks on those who try to stand up for civil rights.

The journey from Atlanta will take place on two buses. A Greyhound bus will leave in the morning on the way to Anniston, Alabama. A Trailways bus will leave in the afternoon that will stop in Birmingham, Alabama.

- To ride the Greyhound bus, turn to page 20.
- To ride the Trailways bus, turn to page 24.

"I'll ride on the Greyhound," you say. Handshakes and nods are exchanged with the group. Then you and Mary return to the dorm to pack. You sense Mary's uncertainty as she sits on the bed.

The next morning, as you prepare to leave, Mary hangs behind. "I don't think I can do it," she says. Your heart sinks, but you understand her concern. She gives you a hug. "Please do it for both of us."

You head to the church, where the two buses wait. You climb aboard the Greyhound, nervous but excited. You sit next to Sam, a white college student. He tells you he was inspired to join the ride by studying the nonviolent protests undertaken by Mahatma Gandhi in India.

"Obviously, this is different," Sam says. "But I want to create change too."

The start of the bus ride is filled with laughter and song. Everyone's spirits are high. But every time the bus rolls through a town, the volume decreases. Riders look carefully out of the windows. In some places, all is quiet. In others, people along the side of the road yell at the bus.

"Some people are curious," Sam says. "Others just want to cause trouble."

Before long, the hum of the bus on the road is the loudest sound. You close your eyes and fall asleep.

"Wake up!" a voice echoes, as you feel a gentle shake. You open your eyes to see Sam standing next to you. "We're pulling into the bus station in Anniston. It looks like we've got company."

Turn the page.

You look out the window and see angry people yelling at the bus. Some are holding torches. Suddenly, a rock hits the window. "Everyone down!" the driver shouts.

As the bus pulls into the station, people quickly move to get off. In the chaos, you get separated from Sam. As you look up, you see him being attacked. Someone throws a homemade bomb onto the bus. Flames burst from the windows, and the mob cheers. Out of the corner of your eye, you see the local police standing by, doing nothing.

One of the experienced riders moves you into a quiet spot. Tears stream down your face.

"We have cars coming to take people to the hospital," he says. "Whoever stays here is likely to go to jail. You can get a ride back to Atlanta, though. It's up to you."

You want to continue helping. But the violence and danger are just too much. When the cars arrive, you sneak into one heading back to school. The bus fire rages in the rearview mirror. The fight will have to go on without you.

THE END

To follow another path, turn to page 10.
To learn more about the fight for the Civil Rights Act of 1964, turn to page 103.

"I'll ride on the Trailways," you say. The group says its goodbyes. Then you and Mary head back to the dorm and pack.

When you get ready to leave the next morning, there's no sign of Mary. You assume she decided to take the Greyhound. When you arrive at the church, the other bus has already left. You push your nerves aside and board the bus.

The mood on the bus is serious. The experienced riders know that danger lies ahead. Because there's an odd number of riders, you're in your own seat. Across from you is Floyd, one of the riders who has been on the trip the entire way.

"It's okay to be a little nervous," he says, reading your mind. "The first ride is always tough. But we have your back."

Floyd goes on to explain how the rides work. There's a mix of observers, who pretend to be regular riders, not part of the movement, and testers. The testers are the people who challenge the law. Black testers sit in the front of the bus, and white testers move to the back. Floyd also explains that at the next stop, they will likely be met by a combination of angry townspeople and the Ku Klux Klan.

"What do we do if we can't fight back?" you wonder.

Floyd answers, "It's difficult." He is quiet for a moment before continuing. "But if we fought back, that would be the story. If the world sees that we are just simply riding the bus and people are attacking us, it helps our cause."

Turn the page.

You nod and ride in silence. You pull out your notebook and start writing down what you've seen. As the bus draws closer to Alabama, tension rises. When you pull into Anniston, everyone on your bus is shocked to see the Greyhound in front of you on fire.

The bus driver slams on the brakes. "Everyone stay put!" he shouts.

Minutes pass as people start banging on the outside of the bus. The driver returns and says, "People on the other bus are going to the hospital. They won't let us move until all the Black riders move to the back of the bus."

"No!" Floyd yells.

You look at the chaos around you. It feels like the breaking point is near. Floyd taps you on the shoulder.

"Now's your chance," he whispers. "We have cars meeting us that can take you back to campus. You can go back to tell our story. Or you can stay with us and finish the ride."

- To head back to campus, turn to page 28.
- To stay on the bus, turn to page 30.

You want to make a difference. But the danger is too real here. You think you can make an impact another way. "I'm going back," you say to Floyd. "But I'll spread the word."

Floyd helps you sneak off the bus and into a waiting car. On the ride back to Atlanta, you start writing down what you experienced as a Freedom Rider. When you get back to campus, you call the editor of the local Black newspaper, the *Atlanta Daily World*.

"I was part of the Freedom Rides," you say. "I think your readers need to know about them."

The editor publishes your story. Letters pour into the paper from readers inspired by the cause. Before long, the editor calls you back into the office.

"We'd like for you to write more articles about the Civil Rights Movement," he says.

This isn't what you imagined for your career, but writing about rallies and protests is exciting. Plus, it helps you feel connected to the movement. You travel to churches, meet with politicians, and talk to everyday people fighting for equality.

"You are helping to give a voice to the voiceless," your editor says. "We can see public opinion starting to shift in our favor."

Writing is an outlet you love. Words can make an impact. You hope that you've made Floyd and the rest of the Freedom Riders proud. You know you'll keep working until real change is made.

THE END

To follow another path, turn to page 10.
To learn more about the fight for the Civil Rights Act of 1964, turn to page 103.

"I'm going to stay with you," you insist. "I'm not scared."

Floyd smiles. He's just about to speak when the bus driver and an angry white man climb aboard.

"This bus isn't going nowhere until all the Black folks move to the back!" he yells.

The Black riders refuse. More white men flood into the bus and throw punches. People scream all around you.

"Stop! You're hurting him!" you yell as one of the older Freedom Riders is pummeled by several Ku Klux Klan members. They turn toward you. You move back a few steps. Floyd steps between you and the men. Before long, all the Freedom Riders have been forced into the back few rows of the bus. Some riders are bruised and bloodied. Everyone is angry.

"Y'all get out of here, now," one of the townspeople says. The driver starts up the bus and rolls out of town. While your group is upset, no one wants to let the mob win. Soon, you are all singing songs of joy and freedom.

After a few hours, the bus pulls into Birmingham. An even bigger mob than the one in Anniston is waiting. There are no police in sight. Klansmen and townspeople attack the riders as you climb off the bus. They scream curse words and slurs. *BAM!* You feel something clang off your head. You stagger into the bus station waiting room in pain.

After an hour of intense back and forth, your group is shuttled to a safe house in the city. You touch the swollen knot on your head as you watch TV coverage of the bus attack. The room goes quiet as the leaders of the ride enter.

Turn the page.

"We've just got word from the head of our organization," one says. "No drivers want to take us any farther. Some of our group is in jail. We're going to have to end the ride here and take a flight to New Orleans."

You're disappointed, but you hope you've made a difference. Surely, the images on TV of peaceful protesters being attacked will change hearts, minds, and, eventually, laws.

THE END

To follow another path, turn to page 10.
To learn more about the fight for the Civil Rights Act of 1964, turn to page 103.

Freedom Riders waiting to board a bus

You've been following the Freedom Riders' journey as best you can on the news. It was heart-breaking watching them get attacked in Alabama. But it was even harder to learn that the ride to New Orleans was going to be stopped after the violent clashes in Birmingham.

"I guess it's all over," you say to Mary.

"Maybe not," she says. "I heard there's a girl in Tennessee who is going to try to keep the Freedom Rides going."

You call your cousin at Fisk University in Nashville. He tells you that a student named Diane Nash is going to restart the ride. She's headed to Birmingham in a few days.

It's a long ride to Nashville but joining this new group of Freedom Riders feels like the right thing to do.

"I'm joining the Freedom Riders," you tell Mary.

"Right now?" she says. "Maybe you should wait a bit. We could get more people to join. Maybe start our own school chapter."

Nash is starting her ride now. Would you rather join her or do the work of starting your own group of riders?

- To join Diane Nash's group in Nashville, turn to page 36.
- To wait and start your ride with a group of friends, turn to page 43.

"I don't want to miss out on this," you tell Mary. "I'm joining Diane Nash's group."

The next morning, you get on the bus to Tennessee. On the long ride, you realize why the Freedom Riders' fight is so important. You're squashed into the back of the bus. At bus stops, you're forced to use poor-quality "colored" restrooms.

When you reach Fisk University, you listen to Nash explain how this group will pick up where the last Freedom Riders left off. The trip to Birmingham will be tough. Nash knows fellow activists who have been hurt, thrown in jail, and had their lives threatened. She gives everyone one final chance to walk away. No one does.

When the bus leaves for Alabama the next morning, you're sitting up front. You've never seen this viewpoint, but it's not that special. Why are white people holding on to it so tightly?

The ride to Birmingham is relatively quiet. But as the bus pulls into the depot, there is a line of police waiting. You recognize Birmingham's notorious commissioner, Eugene "Bull" Connor, standing with a club in his hand.

As soon you all step off the bus, your entire group is arrested and taken to jail. You sing the entire way there. In the holding pen, the group discusses your options. You could pay your bail and be let out. But part of the strategy is to overcrowd the jail to earn publicity for the cause. Police want the riders to leave town as fast as possible. What will you do?

•To get released from jail, turn to page 38.

• To stay in jail, turn to page 41.

Being free gives you another opportunity to act, rather than wait for help. You and several others pay your bail. Bull Connor wants you out of his state. His men drive the group to the Tennessee state line and drop you off. Plans are immediately made to return to Birmingham and challenge the law once again.

Despite the dangers, you commit to the ride for the long term. Your travels take you from Alabama to Mississippi. You get to witness speeches from some of the Civil Rights Movement's biggest leaders, including Dr. Martin Luther King Jr.

The media coverage of your rides and the violence you face continues to spread. People around the country and across the globe watch in horror as innocent riders are confronted by white mobs.

Public opinion turns toward your cause. Finally, the government is ready to act. On November 1, 1961, under heavy pressure from Attorney General Robert Kennedy, the Interstate Commerce Commission (ICC) enacts new policies. Now Black passengers can sit wherever they want on buses and trains. Segregated bathrooms, water fountains, and waiting rooms are removed from terminals. It's a huge step for equal rights.

Political leaders in 1963, including Martin Luther King, Robert Kennedy, and Lyndon Johnson

Turn the page.

"We did it!" you shout to your fellow riders. The ride back home will be unlike any you've ever had. And while it will take a few more years for the Civil Rights Act of 1964 to be passed, ensuring that discrimination is illegal in all aspects of life, this is a key victory. It opens a lot of eyes across the country about how racism is persistent in Black life.

THE END

To follow another path, turn to page 10.
To learn more about the fight for the Civil Rights Act of 1964, turn to page 103.

Part of the group's strategy is to fill the jails with riders who have been unfairly arrested. You use the media coverage of this to draw attention to the rides. "I'll stay in jail," you volunteer. You and three other riders remain inside the Birmingham jail. The authorities just want the Freedom Riders to be someone else's problem, so they shuttle those who paid bail to the state line.

Jail is awful. You never get to go outside. Every time you start to fall asleep, a guard makes a racket to keep you awake. You and your friends sing songs to keep your spirits up and show your strength to the guards.

A few days later, more people join you in the jail. They are battered and bruised.

"We heard the authorities are going to move us to a maximum-security facility," a man named William says. "It's supposed to be brutal there."

Turn the page.

You are worried. This small city jail is one thing. Moving to a real prison is another.

The next morning, the sheriff appears. "I've got something special for y'all," he says. "You're moving to Parchman prison with the rest of the troublemakers."

When they open the cell, the riders are given two choices—go to Parchman or pay bail and leave the state. You want to help the fight, but prison terrifies you. You go back to school. There, you'll work on the outside to free your friends and continue the fight for civil rights.

THE END

To follow another path, turn to page 10.
To learn more about the fight for the Civil Rights Act of 1964, turn to page 103.

"Okay, let's form our own group," you say. In the next few weeks, you and Mary work alongside other students. You build awareness about the Freedom Riders and set up your own ride.

Turn the page.

You become friendly with a student named John. He helps you get a bus and plan a route. Federal government officials have urged groups like yours to consider a cooling-off period. They want a break from the rides, but all the organizations plan on moving forward.

Your ride is scheduled to begin in July. The plan is do drive toward Jackson, Mississippi, one of the biggest hot spots for racial segregation on bus routes.

When you get on the bus the next morning, spirits are high. You have twenty riders on the bus. Most of them are students from your college, but a few are from up North. The mood is upbeat as you make your way toward Jackson.

When you get closer, John stands up and speaks. "We're approaching town," he says. "Expect a rude greeting. Remember our training. Let them arrest us if that's what they want to do."

You couldn't have arrived at a worse possible time. There's another bus at the depot surrounded by angry men. The driver pulls up behind it, and people start getting off. Quickly, John is dragged away by the mob, while other passengers are grabbed by police officers.

• To try to help John, turn to page 46.
• To help others being arrested, turn to page 48.

"John!" you scream as he's pulled away. People are swinging clubs and throwing fists. But John just covers his head. He refuses to fight back.

"You're hurting him!" you yell. The surging crowd knocks you to the ground. You lose sight of John in the madness. Another passenger pulls you to your feet. He has blood trickling from his forehead.

"Are you okay?" you ask. The man nods and moves on to help others.

You turn and search for John. You see a figure on the side of the road.

"John! John! Can you hear me?" John is bloodied, and it looks like he may have broken his arm. You wave down another friend.

"We've got to help John!" you shout to the man. He turns and searches for anyone who can possibly help. A white man approaches as you yell.

"I can take y'all in the back of my pickup," he says.

You quickly agree. You want to make sure your friend is safe, and right now, that's more important than the ride. You can only hope that people see what happened here and decide to help fight for change.

THE END

To follow another path, turn to page 10.
To learn more about the fight for the Civil Rights Act of 1964, turn to page 103.

You rush over to the bus station, where police officers are handcuffing your friends.

"What's going on?" you demand of an officer.

"You're all under arrest," he sneers, motioning for an officer to cuff you. Tears well in your eyes as your hands are roughly put behind your back and the click of the cuffs comes together.

Police arrest a protester.

Your group is gathered and thrown into the back of a paddy wagon. It's a short drive to the county jail. There, men are placed in one holding cell and women in another.

Everyone is figuring out next steps when an officer calls your name. "You've been bailed out," he says. Shocked, you walk to the front of the building, where a woman is waiting for you.

"My name is Claire," she says. "I know you were leading this ride. I work for Womanpower Unlimited. We help Freedom Riders such as yourself."

You and Claire head to the Womanpower office. There, she explains how this woman-led organization provides aid to Freedom Riders and supports the Civil Rights Movement.

"I'm hoping you will join us," Claire says.

Turn the page.

"You help the rest of my group get out of jail, and I'm in," you reply.

The two of you make a deal. Working behind the scenes is a safer, more strategic way to make a difference. You can't wait to get started.

THE END

To follow another path, turn to page 10.
To learn more about the fight for the Civil Rights Act of 1964, turn to page 103.

Civil rights leaders Gloria Richardson and Dr. Rosa Slade Gragg

CHAPTER 3

FOCUS ON BIRMINGHAM

It's 1963, and you live in Birmingham, Alabama, one of the most racially divided cities in the United States. The Civil Rights Movement is trying to change cities like this.

Here, Black and white people rarely interact. Segregation is the norm. Black citizens who try to stand up for themselves are often met with violence from white citizens or the authorities.

Turn the page.

Almost 40 percent of Birmingham is Black. Yet the city has no Black police officers, bus drivers, or cashiers. Only about 10 percent of the Black population is even registered to vote. The Ku Klux Klan make it nearly impossible for them to cast a vote. That makes it just as difficult to change things.

You are a young Black man who has returned to your hometown after graduating college.

You want to help create change, and the Birmingham campaign is doing that with boycotts and sit-ins. You're just afraid they will lead to violence like you've seen on the news. You have just graduated with a teaching degree. Perhaps the best way to spark change is by teaching the next generation.

• To join the Birmingham Campaign, go to the next page.
• To become a teacher, turn to page 66.

You head to a church meeting led by Fred Shuttlesworth. He's the head of the Alabama Christian Movement for Human Rights (ACMHR). The group is joining forces with Dr. Martin Luther King Jr.'s Southern Christian Leadership Conference (SCLC). They're creating an organized, nonviolent plan to end segregation in the city.

Fred Shuttlesworth and Dr. Martin Luther King Jr.

Turn the page.

There's a large crowd of people eager to hear the plan. Shuttlesworth says the goal is to cripple Birmingham's downtown area through a boycott of stores and sit-ins at lunch counters.

"We've got to hit them where it hurts—their wallets," Shuttlesworth says to applause.

A man nudges you in the side. "My name is Maurice," he says. "Forget all this sit-in stuff. We need some action! We need to take it to the man. We need protests, marches, rocks through windows! What do you say, brother?"

You are conflicted. You've heard about how sit-ins and boycotts can help because it hurts the economy. But it may be too low-key for a city like Birmingham. Racism and segregation are such a major element of the city. It may take more drastic action to result in real change.

• To march in downtown, go to the next page.
• To participate in the sit-ins, turn to page 59.

"I'm in for some action," you say to Maurice.

Maurice is excited. You make plans to meet for the upcoming march led by Dr. King through Birmingham. The march brings you face-to-face with some of the city's most vocal segregationists.

On the day of the march, Dr. King stresses that it will be a nonviolent protest. But you can tell Maurice won't back down if he's confronted.

"Remember to keep your cool," you remind Maurice.

The march begins without incident. You and Maurice are in a large group of people toward the back. You can see TV cameras and reporters tracking the march. Just as you reach downtown, someone throws a rock into the group. It hits Maurice. He steps forward and yells in anger.

Turn the page.

That's all it takes for chaos to break out. Police swarm the marchers, striking innocent people with their batons. Snarling police dogs bite screaming protestors.

You watch in horror as Maurice falls to the ground under heavy blows. When the police move on, you drag him to the sidewalk. He is badly hurt.

Later that evening, after taking Maurice to the hospital, you decide to leave Birmingham. You can fight for civil rights from somewhere else. You're afraid you'll lose your life if you continue to do it here.

THE END

To follow another path, turn to page 10.
To learn more about the fight for the Civil Rights Act of 1964, turn to page 103.

You think the sit-ins are the best way to impact the community. The next day, you're standing with a group of five volunteers outside the busiest lunch counter in Birmingham.

"They won't serve us here," says Joseph, the group leader. "But let's sit as long as possible, so other people can't get a seat. Keep your cool."

You swallow hard as the door opens with a *ting* from the bell above it. Heads snap your way as the group heads for the lunch counter.

"Not this again," the cook says. "I told y'all before. We don't serve your kind here!"

The group sits at the empty stools. Joseph speaks calmly to the cook. "I'd like a soda, please," he says. The cook pretends he doesn't hear and turns his back to the group. The white people seated at the counter quickly gather their belongings and move.

Turn the page.

For a long time, things are quiet. You're sitting next to a young woman who is looking straight ahead with a fierce determination.

"My name is Elizabeth, in case you're wondering," she says.

You introduce yourself. Just then, a group of angry customers comes up behind you.

"It's time to leave," one of them says. Another spits at the group. It lands on your face. Elizabeth uses her handkerchief to wipe it off. "Stay calm," she says.

• To remain calm, go to the next page.
• To stand up to the bullies, turn to page 63.

You ignore the violation. After a while, the men leave. As the lunch counter prepares to close, your group calmly walks out of the restaurant while white shoppers insult you.

"That was intense," Joseph says when you're out. "Great job staying calm, y'all."

As the group walks back to the church to report on the day, you and Elizabeth strike up a conversation. You discover that she is a recent college graduate as well.

Before long, you're spending all your free time with Elizabeth. Together, you work on the Birmingham campaign, but also discuss bigger topics.

One day, she says, "I'm going to leave for Washington, D.C., soon. There's going to be a major march up there. Will you come with me?"

Turn the page.

You don't hesitate in saying yes. You'll be thrilled to march side by side with someone you've connected with in the hope of a brighter future.

THE END

To follow another path, turn to page 10.
To learn more about the fight for the Civil Rights Act of 1964, turn to page 103.

You've had enough. You stand up and push the closest man to you. Joseph and Elizabeth quickly pull you back to your stool. But your actions are exactly what the bullies want.

"I told you to stay cool," Joseph whispers.

"I'm sorry," you say quietly.

Before long, sirens blare outside the restaurant. Two angry cops come for you.

Black protesters at a lunch counter

Turn the page.

"You're under arrest," one officers says.

Joseph tries to speak, but the cops raise their batons. "Do you want to get arrested too?" one asks him. You shake your head at Joseph. You made the mistake, and you'll pay the price.

At the jail, you're placed in a cell with many other civil rights activists. Instead of disappointment, there's almost a level of excitement in the holding area.

"Did you hear?" a man whispers. "Dr. King was arrested. He's being held here too."

The news is surprising. Dr. King has done so much for the cause. You hope he's released soon. As you wait for your father to come with bail money, a janitor comes up to the cell.

"Does anyone have any paper?" he asks quietly, looking around. "Dr. King wants to write a letter."

You check your jacket pocket. You do have one neatly folded sheet inside. Elizabeth's name and number is written on one corner. You tear off her number and hand the paper to the guard.

You're proud to help Dr. King in any way you can. Little did you know that your scrap of paper will be part of a historical document. Dr. King's "Letter from a Birmingham Jail" becomes a major call for action for the Civil Rights Movement.

THE END

To follow another path, turn to page 10.
To learn more about the fight for the Civil Rights Act of 1964, turn to page 103.

You get a job as a teacher at the local high school. The facilities are poor, and the books are out of date. But the students are eager to learn, and you're excited to teach them.

The city is buzzing with the efforts of the Birmingham Campaign. There have been some major strides. But it's also been tough. Some of your friends and family have been thrown in jail. Even Dr. Martin Luther King Jr. was arrested! Some people are scared to continue the campaign.

One day, a fellow teacher named Percy is talking to you about the campaign.

"Have you heard of James Bevel?" Percy asks.

You have. He's a young SCLC organizer working on the Birmingham Campaign. But some of his methods have been controversial.

"I hear he's thinking about using kids to march next week," Percy says. "He's calling it the Children's Crusade."

You're caught off guard by the news. Using children in marches could be very dangerous. You care about the kids you teach. You hate to think of anything happening to them. On the other hand, the idea is brilliant. You hope white people wouldn't attack children. But if they did, the media coverage would definitely bring more people to your cause.

• To help with the Children's Crusade, turn to page 68.
• To skip the Children's Crusade, turn to page 75.

When you speak to your class the next day, they are excited about participating in a march. You tell them that James Bevel has organized meetings so they can learn about nonviolent protests. You warn your students about the dangers they may face. You urge them to speak to their parents before marching.

James Bevel

"Just know that if you join this fight and fail, the powerful people in town will not let you forget it," you tell your students. "They could make your life miserable."

You know that a seventh grader named Gwendolyn Sanders is organizing a walkout of the school to take part in the march on May 2. While most students are eager to join the cause, some are hesitant.

After class, a boy named Charles shyly approaches your desk.

"What should I do?" he says. "I want to participate, but I'm scared. I talked to my parents, and they said it was my choice. But I'm still nervous. I was hoping you might give me some advice."

- To encourage Charles to take part on May 2, turn to page 70.
- To suggest Charles, wait and see what happens, turn to page 72.

"Charles, I think it would be a great idea to participate," you say. "I know you kids can really make an impact." Charles smiles and thanks you as he leaves the classroom. You hope you've given him the right advice.

On the day of the march, you're stunned to see hundreds of children, some as young as seven years old, ready to fight for their rights. Kids are singing, laughing, and working with adults to strategize their movements.

Clusters of children start making their way downtown. You keep an eye on Charles as he walks in front of you, singing "We Shall Overcome."

As soon as the groups reach the city, however, the police are waiting. You look on in horror as children are arrested and placed in school buses for a trip to jail. Still, the mood never changes. It's almost a joyous scene.

As they are being arrested, children speak to reporters to tell them why they joined the cause. Charles tells a reporter, "I want my kids to grow up in a world where they can go where they want and do what they want."

About 1,000 children are arrested. They fill the Birmingham City Jail. When you catch up with Charles, he has a smile on his face.

"It was worth it," he says. "I'm going to keep organizing and marching until we have our rights."

THE END

To follow another path, turn to page 10.
To learn more about the fight for the Civil Rights Act of 1964, turn to page 103.

You're leery of sending a child into possible danger. "Why don't you wait and see what happens after the first day of the march," you suggest to Charles, sensing his hesitation.

"Thanks, sir," he says. "I think I will."

The first day of the march is a success, despite hundreds of children being arrested. The media coverage of children being arrested has angered people around the world.

You head down for the second day of the Children's Crusade. There's a much larger police presence than the day before. They're clustered at the 16th Street Baptist Church, where everyone has congregated.

When the march begins, the police and firefighters start shouting. Then they turn on the fire hoses. A powerful stream of water knocks you to the ground.

You scramble to help kids as they are hit with a high-pressure jet. As the onlookers protest, the police release their attack dogs on the crowd.

You look up to see the commissioner of public safety, Bull Connor, laughing at the chaos. You're angry, hurt, and scared. You find Charles. He is crouched behind a car, protecting a young girl.

Black children are sprayed with high-powered hoses during the Children's Crusade.

Turn the page.

"Are you okay, Charles?" you ask. He nods.

After several hours, the water stops, and the dogs are leashed. People start leaving. You take Charles home, thankful he's not seriously hurt. The fight for civil rights is critical, but you wonder whether putting children in harm's way is worth it.

THE END

To follow another path, turn to page 10.
To learn more about the fight for the Civil Rights Act of 1964, turn to page 103.

After a lot of thought, you decide to stay behind with the children whose parents don't want them to participate in the Children's Crusade. You won't be part of putting children in harm's way.

Protesters run from dogs and fire hoses.

Turn the page.

You try to teach some lessons, but the children are distracted. They are worried about what's happening with their friends. Some are upset they didn't get to protest. Others are too young to understand what's going on.

"Why do the white folks hate us?" one child asks you. You don't have a good answer.

That night, you talk with your parents about what's happening in the city.

"What do you think I should do?" you ask. "I can't go on living as a second-class citizen. I want to help fix things, but I also want to feel safe and free. I don't think I can do that in Birmingham."

Your parents understand your frustration. But they urge you to stick around and help make your hometown a better place.

• To leave the city, go to the next page.
• To stay in the city, turn to page 79.

"I don't think I can deal with this anymore," you say. "I'm going to visit Uncle David up in Detroit and see if I can get settled there."

It's hard leaving Birmingham, but there are opportunities to live a better life. And the fight for civil rights in the North isn't as dangerous as it is in the South. You are not the only Black person to move for better economic opportunities and social conditions. Nearly six million Black people from Southern states move to other parts of the country. The movement is called the Great Migration.

You continue to follow what happens in Birmingham in the news. You are thrilled to see that the Children's Crusade has helped spur change in the city. However, you wake up on the morning of September 15, 1963, to horrible news.

Turn the page.

The Ku Klux Klan bombed the 16th Street Baptist Church in Birmingham, killing four young girls inside. One of them had been a student of yours. Tears stream down your face as you wonder if Birmingham will ever change.

THE END

To follow another path, turn to page 10.
To learn more about the fight for the Civil Rights Act of 1964, turn to page 103.

Your parents are right. You can't expect others to fight while you flee. You stay in Birmingham and attend a meeting hosted by SCLC leader Fred Shuttlesworth. He was injured in the protest by water from a fire hose.

"You have to be prepared to die before you can live in freedom," Shuttlesworth says.

The message hits home for you. You spend several weeks working hard on the campaign. You participate in sit-ins at the local lunch counter. You help organize protests in front of the church. Slowly, it seems like change is on the horizon. The city and civil rights leaders come to an agreement. Birmingham would desegregate. "Whites" and "Colored" signs would be taken down. Companies and government organizations would be required to hire Black workers. The news was met with celebration across the community.

Turn the page.

"We did it!" your mother shouts. "I never thought I would see the day."

But the victory is short-lived. Three months later, the outward signs of discrimination are gone, but you still don't see any Black officers or clerks. Bombings still terrorize Black communities. You know racism won't disappear overnight, but you're ready to do everything you can to get Black citizens on equal ground in Birmingham.

THE END

To follow another path, turn to page 10.
To learn more about the fight for the Civil Rights Act of 1964, turn to page 103.

THIS SCULPTURE IS DEDICATED TO THE
FOOT SOLDIERS OF THE BIRMINGHAM
CIVIL RIGHTS MOVEMENT.

WITH GALLANTRY, COURAGE AND GREAT
BRAVERY THEY FACED THE VIOLENCE
OF ATTACK DOGS, HIGH POWERED WATER
HOSES, AND BOMBINGS. THEY WERE
THE FODDER IN THE ADVANCE AGAINST
INJUSTICE. WARRIORS OF A JUST CAUSE;
THEY REPRESENT HUMANITY UNSHAKEN
IN THEIR FIRM BELIEF IN THEIR NATION'S
COMMITMENT TO LIBERTY AND JUSTICE
FOR ALL.

WE SALUTE THESE MEN AND WOMEN
WHO WERE THE SOLDIERS OF THIS GREAT
CAUSE.

1995   RONALD S. McDOWELL, ARTIST I.B.I.C.

In May 1995, a sculpture was put up in Birmingham, dedicated to "the foot soldiers of the Birmingham Civil Rights Movement."

CHAPTER 4

MARCH TOWARD HISTORY

It's 1963, and the Civil Rights Movement is building. From Freedom Riders to child protestors, people from all walks of life have been working against discrimination and fighting for equal rights.

But the movement is scattered. There are marches in the South. There are meetings in the North. What's needed is a national course of action to help spur President John F. Kennedy to enact meaningful civil rights laws.

Turn the page.

In the aftermath of violent clashes in Birmingham, Alabama, in 1963, there is a push to make a peaceful statement. The goal is to bring the best and brightest civil rights leaders together for one major project.

You are a Black woman who works at a doctor's office in New York City. One of your co-workers recently informed you that Dr. Martin Luther King Jr. and others are planning a big march in Washington, D.C., later this summer.

"That sounds interesting," you say. "I wonder how I can get involved?"

- To help organize the march, go to the next page.
- To simply participate in the march, turn to page 94.

You want to help in any way you can. You learn that the organizers behind the march are A. Philip Randolph and Bayard Rustin. These activists want to bring together civil rights leaders to create a unified front. They've set up an office in New York City as a headquarters.

A. Philip Randolph

Turn the page.

You want to be part of this historical movement. When you arrive at march headquarters, people of all races, genders, and ages are gathered.

The woman sitting next to you reaches out her hand. "My name is Joan," she says.

You smile and shake her hand. You've never had a white person be friendly with you. You both listen as Rustin begins detailing the volunteer jobs. They include passing out pamphlets, raising money, building public support, and organizing transportation.

"Let's work together!" Joan says. "What should we do?"

• To pass out pamphlets, go to the next page.
• To help with other aspects, turn to page 89.

"Let's pass out pamphlets to teach people why the march is so important," you say.

You and Joan get a large stack of the pamphlets. They explain that the march is about equal rights and job creation for all. They also say that the march is a nonviolent protest featuring speakers and musicians. Bullet points on the pamphlet explain the desire for desegregation in schools and a minimum wage for all.

You've been assigned to pass out pamphlets in the Bronx, one of New York City's five boroughs. The day starts out well. You and Joan discover that most people are genuinely interested in the march. But as you move through the neighborhood, you notice that you are being followed by a police officer. You whisper to Joan that perhaps it's time to wrap up for the day.

"What are you ladies doing?" he asks sternly.

Turn the page.

"We're handing out flyers for the March on Washington," you say, handing him one. He looks at it and rips it up.

"Do you have a permit to do this?" he sneers. He yanks the bag of flyers off Joan's shoulder and dumps them in a gutter.

"Hey, you can't do that!" Joan yells.

Suddenly, the cop pulls out his baton and strikes Joan on the arm. She crumples to the ground in tears.

"Time for you ladies to leave," he says.

You help Joan to her feet and head to the subway. You want to support the march, but the danger is too much. It's time to go back home where you know you'll be safe.

THE END

To follow another path, turn to page 10.
To learn more about the fight for the Civil Rights Act of 1964, turn to page 103.

"There's so much to organize," you say. "I can use my office skills to help with all the details."

You and Joan go to an office where a large map of the National Mall is hung on the wall. Next to that are several large labels that read, BUSES, PARKING, POLICE, BATHROOMS.

"Bathrooms?" Joan says with a laugh.

"It's no laughing matter," says a volunteer. She points at a stack of letters. "We've been getting letters from senators wondering how we'll provide restrooms and water for 100,000 people. Mr. Rustin is working very hard on it."

Everywhere you turn, people are tackling problems. Phones ring. Shouts fly across the room. Paper is stacked everywhere. How will you help?

• To help coordinate bus transportation, turn to page 90.
• To contact government officials for help, turn to page 92.

"I want to help with the buses," you say. Thousands of buses will be needed to bring people to the march. You also need to organize parking for all the vehicles. It's hard work, but you spend the next few weeks calling bus companies around the country, securing transportation.

You're thrilled when the United Auto Workers union tells you that they are financing bus travel for 5,000 of its members. You've also helped get 450 buses to take marchers from New York City to Washington.

"Our final hurdle for transportation is the Midwest," your supervisor says one day.

"My cousin is a bus driver in Chicago," you reply. "I will get him to help."

Your cousin agrees to get you 50 buses. You thank him and run to tell your supervisor.

Protesters arrive at the March on Washington.

"This is great," he says. "We've reached our goal!"

The whole office cheers. When the march begins, you'll be proud to have played a part in everyone getting there safely.

THE END

To follow another path, turn to page 10.
To learn more about the fight for the Civil Rights Act of 1964, turn to page 103.

"I would like to reach out to government officials," you say. You're given a script to follow on the phone and a form letter to mail.

It's difficult work because it's hard to contact the state officials, politicians, and other business leaders the march wants to get on its side. Some people hang up almost instantly. But a few are willing to talk. They have lots of questions about what the goals are for the march.

Fortunately, Rustin has created and distributed a manual that answers nearly everything anyone could ask. You memorize the manual and can discuss it with anyone.

As the event gets closer, you get a call at your desk.

"Is this the headquarters for the March on Washington?" the voice asks.

When you say yes, he replies, "Good. I've just planted a bomb there. I'm going to blow you all up!"

You put down the phone and run to your supervisor to report the threat. The entire building clears out. After the police search the building, they determine the call was fake.

You're shaken up. But you're even more convinced that the March on Washington is the event this country needs to create change.

THE END

To follow another path, turn to page 10.
To learn more about the fight for the Civil Rights Act of 1964, turn to page 103.

After months of reading about the March on Washington, you decide to take part in the historic event. You sign up for a bus trip to Washington.

When you arrive at the bus terminal, you're shocked to see dozens of buses lined up. Thousands of people wait to start the journey.

When you finally make it on a bus, some people are happy, and others are nervous. No one knows what will happen when you make it to Washington.

The ride begins with the entire bus singing. Eventually, a steady silence takes over as people begin reading or sleeping.

"My name is Adam," says the young man seated next to you. "Why are you going to Washington?"

People board buses for the March on Washington.

You explain to him that you've been energized by the Civil Rights Movement and want to show the world that Black people deserve equal rights and fair opportunities.

Turn the page.

Adam tells you that he's from the South, where Jim Crow laws have made it impossible for him and his family to live a good life.

You and Adam chat for a long time and discover that you have many things in common. You make plans to walk together in Washington. You're happy to have a friend on this journey.

Just as you settle in for a nap, the bus jolts to a stop on the side of the road. After a few minutes, the driver says the bus needs repairs, but another bus will be along in little while. Some of you can squeeze in with them. Everyone groans and gets off. You watch as Adam chats with the people in a nearby car. He jogs over to you, excited.

"These people are going to the March," he says. "They offered to give us a ride. What do you say?"

• To accept the ride, go to the next page.
• To stay with the bus, turn to page 100.

You hesitate for a second. Adam notices. "I promise it will be safe. They're a young married couple," he says.

"Okay, let's do it," you say. "Who knows how long it will take to fix the bus. I don't want to be late."

You get into the car and are introduced to the couple, Patricia and Gregory. The ride is fun, as you all discuss who's supposed to appear at the march. You wonder aloud whether President Kennedy will sign a law ensuring civil rights.

The ride is smooth for a long time. But as you start getting closer to Washington, traffic builds up. The sheer number of buses on the road makes it difficult for cars to get through.

"Are we going to make it on time?" you wonder.

Turn the page.

Gregory tries to take a different route to avoid traffic. At first, it works well. Without all the buses on the road, you're able to drive much faster. But then Gregory makes a wrong turn. Before long, you're on side roads heading away from Washington.

Gregory pulls the car over to study the map, and everyone gets out to stretch their legs. You are worried that you won't make it there in time.

"This is really important to me—to all of us," you say to Adam.

When you get back in the car, the ride is tense. Gregory tries to make up lost time. But when you arrive in D.C., the March has already started.

"We missed it!" Patricia says, disappointed.

"I think it's still going," you say. "Let's hurry over there."

Somehow, you make your way through the massive crowd and find a small space at the edge just in time to hear someone announce Dr. Martin Luther King Jr.!

You may have missed most of the march, but you hear Dr. King's iconic "I Have A Dream" speech. It's a moment you'll never forget.

THE END

To follow another path, turn to page 10.
To learn more about the fight for the Civil Rights Act of 1964, turn to page 103.

You don't know Adam well, and you don't know these new people at all. You're willing to wait for another bus to be on the safe side. When it finally arrives, you squeeze onto the new bus.

When you climb aboard, you're in for a shock—the bus is primarily made up of white people! One white man offers you his seat. That's a first for you! You're happy to take a seat after being outside for several hours, but you can't help feeling like this is some kind of trick.

"I'm sorry," you say to the man seated on the floor next to you. "Are you all going to the March on Washington?"

The man laughs. "That's right. Name's Jack. Most of us are auto workers from Detroit. There are some church folks on here too. We want to do our part to help."

You nod in agreement. When the bus reaches Washington, everyone decides to stick together and march. Your group is one of the largest integrated gatherings at the march.

"This is how it should be," you say to Jack as you walk toward the National Mall. "People of all kinds working together to make a difference."

You stand and listen to the speakers with a smile on your face. Dr. King speaks of his dream where one day, people are judged by the content of their character and not the color of their skin. You feel a real hope that his dream is one day closer to coming true.

THE END

To follow another path, turn to page 10.
To learn more about the fight for the Civil Rights Act of 1964, turn to page 103.

CHAPTER 5

CIVIL RIGHTS ACT OF 1964: YEARS IN THE MAKING

On July 2, 1964, President Lyndon B. Johnson signed the Civil Rights Act into law. This long overdue measure banned segregation based on race, religion, sex, or national origin at all public places. This included schools, parks, restaurants, theaters, and hotels. Black people and other minorities could no longer be denied service based on race.

The act also banned discrimination by employers and labor unions based on race, religion, and gender. After years of sit-ins, Freedom Rides, protests, and the March on Washington, the Civil Rights Movement had accomplished a landmark victory.

Dr. Martin Luther King Jr. called the passage of the law a "second Emancipation Proclamation." He was referring to President Abraham Lincoln's Emancipation Proclamation that freed the slaves.

In the aftermath of the Civil Rights Act, schools began to integrate. This gave Black children an opportunity for an equal education. Black workers finally had the chance to compete for better paying jobs. And even something as simple as riding the bus became a more pleasant experience.

The Civil Rights Act also opened the door for two other major pieces of legislation. The Voting Rights Act of 1965 ensured voting protections. The Civil Rights Act of 1968 helped with housing equality and new laws against racially motivated violence.

These bills did not end racism or the fight for justice. But they were huge steps in the journey toward equality. The fight continues today through movements to ensure Black, women's, LGBTQIA+, Latinx, and Indigenous rights.

President Johnson signs the Voting Rights Act of 1965.

Timeline of the Civil Rights Movement

January 1, 1863: The Emancipation Proclamation is announced by President Abraham Lincoln, releasing all enslaved people in the Confederacy. However, with the Civil War still being fought, none are actually freed at that time.

January 31, 1865: Congress passes the 13th Amendment to the Constitution, abolishing enslavement in the United States.

1880s: Jim Crow laws legalize racial segregation on a state and local level throughout the South.

1941: A. Philip Randolph and Bayard Rustin plan the original March on Washington to pressure President Franklin D. Roosevelt to open military hiring to Black men. The march is canceled when Roosevelt agrees to a deal.

February 1, 1960: The first sit-ins occur when four Black students from North Carolina Agricultural and Technical College sit at a lunch counter at a local store and refuse to leave.

May 4, 1961: The first Freedom Riders bus leaves Washington, D.C., to challenge segregated public transportation.

April 12, 1963: Dr. Martin Luther King Jr. is arrested in Birmingham while protesting the city's rampant segregation. He writes his "Letter from a Birmingham Jail" while imprisoned.

May 2–3, 1963: The Children's Crusade uses school-aged children to march against segregation. About 2,000 are arrested, and others are injured by police.

August 28, 1963: More than 250,000 people attend the March on Washington, highlighted by Dr. King's "I Have A Dream" speech. Freedom Rider John Lewis also spoke at the event. At only twenty-three years old, he was the youngest speaker at the event. Lewis went on to become a U.S. Congressman.

July 2, 1964: The Civil Rights Act of 1964 is passed. It is followed by the Voting Rights Act of 1965 and the Civil Rights Act of 1968 to form the three most important civil rights laws.

Other Paths to Explore

1. Imagine you are a Black parent. Your child wants to be part of the Children's Crusade. You support the cause of equality, but you fear for your child's safety. Would you support them in their decision to take part? Why or why not?

2. You are a Jewish rabbi in New York, and some members of your congregation have approached you to discuss the parallels between the civil rights violence and the atrocities committed against Jewish people throughout history. Should you make the tough choice and stand with Black people to help achieve civil rights, or do you think it is not your fight?

3. You are a white factory worker in Birmingham. You're happy that they changed the laws so that Black workers can get decent jobs. But now you're noticing the supervisors creating a test that only Black workers have to pass to get jobs like yours. You've seen the test, and it's very difficult. You don't think you could pass it. Do you speak up and tell your boss this isn't fair? Or is this problem too big for you to handle?

Glossary

activist (AK-tih-vuhst)—a person who works for social or political change

boycott (BOY-kot)—to refuse to buy or use a product or service to protest something believed to be wrong or unfair

civil rights (SIH-vuhl RITES)—legal rights guaranteed to every citizen of a country relating to such things as voting and receiving equal treatment

discrimination (dis-kri-muh-NAY-shuhn)—the act of treating people unfairly because of their race, country of birth, or gender

editor (EH-duh-tur)—the person who is in charge of a newspaper

Jim Crow laws (JIM KROH LAWZ)—a series of laws in Southern states designed to keep white people and Black people separate and to limit the freedom of Black people

racism (RAY-si-zim)—the belief that one race is better than another race

segregation (seg-ruh-GAY-shuhn)—the practice of keeping groups of people apart, especially based on race

Bibliography

An Oral History of the March on Washington
smithsonianmag.com/history/oral-history-march-washington-180953863/

Birmingham Campaign
kinginstitute.stanford.edu/encyclopedia/birmingham-campaign

Person, Charles. *Buses Are a Comin': Memoir of a Freedom Rider.* New York: Saint Martin's Press. 2021.

The Children's Crusade: When the Youth of Birmingham Marched for Justice
history.com/news/childrens-crusade-birmingham-civil-rights

The Civil Rights Act of 1964. United States National Archives
archives.gov/milestone-documents/civil-rights-act

Read More

Doeden, Matt. *John Lewis: Courage in Action*. Minneapolis: Lerner Publications, 2018.

Joy, Angela. *Choosing Brave: Mamie Till-Mobley, Emmett Till, and the Voice that Sparked the Civil Rights Movement*. New York: Roaring Brook Press, 2022.

Leslie, Jay. *The Rise: 1967*. New York: Franklin Watts, an imprint of Scholastic Inc., 2023.

Internet Sites

African-American Civil Rights Movement
historyforkids.net/african-american-civil-rights.html

Civil Rights Movement
kids.britannica.com/students/article/civil-rights-movement/310706

National Civil Rights Museum Student Resources
civilrightsmuseum.org/students

JOIN OTHER HISTORICAL ADVENTURES WITH MORE
YOU CHOOSE SEEKING HISTORY!

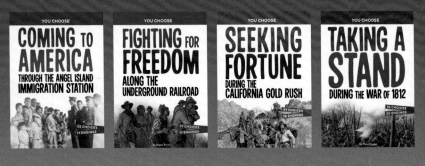

About the Author

Elliott Smith is an author and freelance writer who has written more than 60 children's books, both fiction and nonfiction, on a variety of subjects, including history, sports, and modern issues. He lives in the Washington, D.C., area with his wife and two children.